T0273124

In Defense of Empires

THE HENRY WENDT LECTURE SERIES

The Henry Wendt Lecture is delivered annually at the American Enterprise Institute by a scholar who has made major contributions to our understanding of the modern phenomenon of globalization and its consequences for social welfare, government policy, and the expansion of liberal political institutions. The lecture series is part of AEI's Wendt Program in Global Political Economy, established through the generosity of the SmithKline Beecham pharmaceutical company (now Glaxo SmithKline) and Mr. Henry Wendt, former chairman and chief executive officer of SmithKline Beecham and trustee emeritus of AEI.

GROWTH AND INTERACTION IN THE WORLD ECONOMY:
THE ROOTS OF MODERNITY
Angus Maddison

IN DEFENSE OF EMPIRES
Deepak Lal

THE POLITICAL ECONOMY OF WORLD MASS MIGRATION:
COMPARING TWO GLOBAL CENTURIES
Jeffrey G. Williamson

In Defense of Empires

Deepak Lal

The AEI Press

Publisher for the American Enterprise Institute

WASHINGTON, D.C.

Available in the United States from the AEI Press, c/o Client Distribution Services, 193 Edwards Drive, Jackson, TN 38301. To order, call toll free: 1-800-343-4499. Distributed outside the United States by arrangement with Eurospan, 3 Henrietta Street, London WC2E 8LU, England.

Library of Congress Cataloging-in-Publication Data

Lal, Deepak
    In defense of empires / Deepak Lal.
      p. cm.
    Includes bibliographical references.
    ISBN 978-0-8447-7177-9 (pbk.)
      1. Imperialism. 2. Colonies. 3. Great Britain—Colonies.
    4. United States—Foreign relations—1989- I. Title.

JC359.L294 2004
325'.32—dc22

                                               2004051816
10 09 08 07 06 05 04   1 2 3 4 5

In Defense of Empires
Deepak Lal

Empires have undeservedly gotten a bad name, particularly in America, ever since President Woodrow Wilson proclaimed the end of the Age of Empires and ushered in the Age of Nations. But this was not always so. In an 1881 letter to British Prime Minister William Gladstone, King Bell and King Acqua of the Cameroons River, West Africa, wrote:

> We want to be under Her Majesty's control. We want our country to be governed by British Government. We are tired of governing this country ourselves, every dispute leads to war, and often to great loss of lives, so we think it is best thing to give up the country to you British men who no doubt will bring peace, civilization, and Christianity in the country. . . . We are quite willing to abolish all our heathen customs. . . . No doubt God will bless you for putting a light in our country.[1]

This lecture is based in part on Deepak Lal, "Cultural Self-Determination, Decentralisation and the Growth of Prosperity," in *A Liberating Economic Journey: Essays in Honour of Ljubo Sirc*, eds. A. Brezski and J. Winnecki (London: Centre for Research on Communist Economies, 2000); Deepak Lal, "The Development and Spread of Economic Norms and Incentives," in *The New Great Power Coalition*, ed. R. Rosecrance (Boston: Rowan and Littlefield, 2001); and Deepak Lal, "Globalisation, Imperialism and Regulation," *Cambridge Review of International Affairs* 14, no. 1 (2001): 107–21. It forms part of a forthcoming book, Deepak Lal, *In Praise of Empires: Globalization and Order* (New York: Palgrave Macmillan, 2004).

Gladstone demurred, and Germany snapped up the offer instead. This example provides the major justifications for and against empires. The major argument in favor of empires is that, through their pax, they provide the most basic of public goods—order—in an anarchical international society of states. This is akin to maintaining order in social life. In *The Anarchical Society*, the late Hedley Bull cogently summarized the three basic values of all social life, which any international order should seek to protect: first, that life is secured against violence leading to death or bodily harm; second, that promises once made are kept; and third, that "the possession of things will remain stable to some degree and will not be subject to challenges that are constant and without limit."[2]

Empires—which we can define as "multi-ethnic conglomerates held together by transnational organizational and cultural ties"[3]—have historically both maintained peace and promoted prosperity for a simple reason. The centers of the ancient civilizations in Eurasia, which practiced sedentary agriculture and yielded a surplus to feed the towns, were bordered in the north and south by areas of nomadic pastoralism: the steppes of the north and the semidesert of the Arabian Peninsula to the south. In these regions, the inhabitants had kept up many of the warlike traditions of our hunter-gatherer ancestors and were prone to prey upon the inhabitants of the sedentary plains, at times attempting to convert them into their chattel like cattle.[4] This meant that the provision of one of the classical public goods—protection of citizens from invaders—required the extension of territory to some natural barriers that could keep the barbarians at bay. The Roman, Chinese, and various Indian empires were partly created to provide this pax, which was vital to keeping their labor-intensive and sedentary forms of making a living intact. The pax of various imperia has thus been essential in providing one of the basic public goods required for prosperity.

These empires can be distinguished as either multicultural or homogenizing. The former included the Abbasid, the Ottoman, the Austro-Hungarian, the British, and the various Indian empires, where little attempt was made to change "the habits of the heart" of the constituent groups—or if it was, as in the early British Raj, an ensuing backlash led to a reversal of policy.

The homogenizing empires, by contrast, sought to create a "national" identity out of the multifarious groups in their territory. The best example is China, where the ethnic mix was unified as Hans through the bureaucratic device of writing their names in characters in a Chinese form and suppressing any subsequent discontent through the subtle repression of a bureaucratic authoritarian state.[5] The Han were an ethnic group whose leaders created the Chin dynasty. They created a unified Han identity by making other ethnic groups adopt their language, Mandarin Chinese, which forced them to adopt their Chinese characters for even something as intimate as writing their own names. In our own time, the American "melting pot"—creating Americans out of a multitude of ethnicities by adherence to a shared civic culture and a common language—has resulted in a similar homogenized imperial state. Likewise, the supposedly ancient "nations" of Britain and France were created through a state-led homogenizing process.[6] India, by contrast, is another imperial state whose political unity is a legacy of the British Raj, but whose multiethnic character is underwritten by an ancient hierarchical structure which accommodates these different groups as different castes.

Despite nationalist rhetoric, an imperial pax has usually succeeded in providing this essential public good—order—in the past. Consider an ordinary citizen (of any ethnic and religious origin) of either of the two nineteenth-century empires extinguished by President Wilson at Versailles (the Austro-Hungarian and the Ottoman) who is contemplating the likelihood of his grandchildren living, surviving, and passing on property to their children. Compare him to a citizen of a postimperial successor state pondering the same prospect. There can be no doubt of the great deterioration of opportunities that has befallen the average citizen of the successor states. The situation in many ways is worse in Africa, with its millions of refugees and ethnic slaughter—even if we consider the inhuman and brutal regime of Leopold's Belgian

Empire in the Congo. In many parts of the postimperial world, the main beneficiaries of the Age of Nations have been the "nationalist" predatory elites who have failed to provide even the most elemental of public goods—law and order.

The imperial pax has also historically been associated with globalization—which is not a new phenomenon—and the prosperity it breeds, for two important reasons. First, in the language of institutional economics, transaction costs are reduced by these transnational organizations, through their extension of metropolitan property rights to other countries. Second, by integrating loosely linked or even autarkic countries and regions—through free flows of goods, capital, and people—into a common economic space, empires promote those gains from trade and specialization emphasized by Adam Smith, leading to what I label Smithian intensive growth. Thus the Graeco-Roman empires linked the areas around the Mediterranean; the Abbasid Empire of the Arabs linked the worlds of the Mediterranean and the Indian Ocean; the Mongol Empire linked China with the Near East; the various Indian empires created a common economic space in the subcontinent; and the expanding Chinese Empire linked the economic spaces of the Yellow River with those of the Yangtze. The British were the first to knit the whole world together through their empire. But most of these empires ultimately declined.

Given the existing technology and the inevitable predatoriness of the state, most empires overextended themselves.[7] Though as table 1 (from the late Sam Finer's masterful *History of Government*) shows, most lasted for longer than this ex-colony has existed as an independent state. The decline of empires was followed by a disintegration of the enlarged economic spaces they had created. As Finer notes about the disintegration of the Roman Empire:

> If a peasant family in Gaul, or Spain, or northern Italy had been able to foresee the misery and exploitation that was to befall his grandchildren and their grandchildren, on and on and on for the next 500 years, he would have been singularly spiritless—and witless

TABLE 1

LIFE SPAN OF EMPIRES

Egypt	2580 BC–30 BC	2,820 years
China	221 BC–1912 AD	2,133 years
Venice	687 AD–1799 AD	1,112 years
Rome	509 BC–476 AD	985 years
Byzantine	330 AD–1204 AD	874 years
Assyria	1356 BC–12 BC	744 years
Ottoman	c.1350 AD–1918 AD	568 years
Sassanian Persian Empire	224–651 AD	427 years
Caliphate	632 AD–943 AD	312 years
Achemenian Persian Empire	550–330 BC	220 years
British Empire in India	1757–1947 AD	190 years

SOURCE: S. E. Finer, *The History of Government*, vol. 1 (Oxford: Oxford University Press, 1997), 31–32.

too—if he had not rushed to the aid of the empire. And even then the kingdoms that did finally emerge after the year 1000 were poverty stricken dung heaps compared with Rome. Not till the full Renaissance in the sixteenth century did Europeans begin to think of themselves as in any ways comparable to Rome, and not till the "Augustan Age" of the eighteenth century did they regard their civilization as its equal.[8]

In our own times, the death of the nineteenth-century liberal international economic order (LIEO) built by Pax Britannia on the fields of Flanders led to nearly a century of economic disintegration and disorder, which has only been repaired in the last decade, with the undisputed emergence of the United States as the world leader. But is the United States willing and able to maintain its pax, which will underwrite the resurrection of another LIEO (like the British in the nineteenth century), and if not, what are the likely consequences? These are the central questions to consider.

I

Gladstone's reasons for not acceding to the request of Kings Bell and Acqua of the Cameroons River are still resonant today, not least in the hearts of many classical liberals. For, though Adam Smith did not have much to say about empires per se,[9] his followers Cobden and Bright—the leaders of the anti-imperial party, along with Gladstone, the Liberals' leader—argued that the imperialists' belief that empire was in England's economic interests was false. Even today, economic historians are unable to agree whether or not the benefits of retaining and expanding the formal British Empire after 1850 exceeded its costs.[10] The nineteenth-century classical liberals rightly maintained that, as foreign trade and investment were mutually advantageous (a non-zero-sum game), no empire was needed to obtain these gains from trade. All that was required was free trade and laissez-faire.

Additionally, as these classical liberals (unlike their American cousins) believed in the correct free trade doctrine—that despite other countries' protectionism, unilateral free trade was in the national interest—they did not want an empire to force other countries to free their foreign trade and investment. They successfully urged Britain to unilaterally promote free trade through the repeal of the Corn Laws in 1846. By contrast, the current world leader—the United States—has never accepted the case for unilateral free trade, and has instead insisted on reciprocity, based on the erroneous doctrine that foreign trade is a zero-sum game. This has poisoned the wells against the nascent new imperium.

But these classical liberals went further, believing the interdependence resulting from a world knit by mutually advantageous trade and investment would also lead to universal peace. They projected the spontaneous order of a market economy in which seemingly conflicting interests were unintentionally harmonized onto the international arena. This was the view of the Enlightenment, as codified in Kant's *Perpetual Peace*. The apotheosis of this English Liberalism was Sir Norman Angell's pacifist 1910 book, *The Great Illusion*, which in 1933 won him the Nobel Peace Prize. In the

Liberal tradition, he argues that war is economically irrational, as it imposes excessive fiscal burdens, defeated powers seldom pay indemnities, colonies do not provide a profit, and "trade cannot be destroyed or captured by a military Power." But, "what is the real guarantee of the good behaviour of one state to another? It is the elaborate interdependence which, not only in the economic sense, but in every sense, makes an unwarrantable aggression of one state upon another react upon the interests of the aggressor."[11]

The Liberals, however, did not altogether eschew empire, for as Angell states:

> Where the condition of a territory is such that the social and economic co-operation of other countries with it is impossible, we may expect the intervention of military force, not as the result of the "annexationist illusion," but as the outcome of real social forces pushing to the maintenance of order. That is the story of England in Egypt, or, for that matter, in India. And if America has any justification in the Philippines at all, it is not that she has "captured" these populations by force of conquest, as in the old days a raiding tribe might capture a band of cattle, but that she is doing there a work of police and administration which the natives cannot do for themselves.[12]

This is the "white man's burden" argument for empire, which meant that even Liberals were in favor of an empire to maintain a pax.

It was Woodrow Wilson who questioned this "policing" justification for empire. He was a utopian whose world view was a strange mixture of classical liberalism, Burkean conservatism, Presbyterianism, and socialism.[13] He referred to himself as an imperialist on two occasions, but meaning only a form of economic imperialism, in line with his former student Frederick Jackson Turner, whose frontier thesis "implied that the US required greater foreign markets in order to sustain its prosperity."[14] But "for every sentence he uttered on commerce, he spoke two on the moral responsibility of the United States to sustain its historic idealism and render the service of its democracy."[15] During his campaign for the Democratic presidential nomination in 1912, Wilson said, "I believe that God planted in us visions of liberty . . . that we are chosen . . . to show the way to the nations of the world how they shall walk in the paths of liberty."[16] The instrument for achieving this Utopia was to be the League of Nations, maintaining collective security and bringing transgressors into line through sanctions. The traditional notion of "national interest," which had governed the European balance-of-power system, was eschewed, to be replaced by a community of nation-states in which the weak and the strong would have equal rights. In his new world order, said Wilson, the only questions would be: "Is it right? Is it just? Is it in the interest of mankind?"[17]

This Wilsonian moralistic universalism was countered by the isolationist Jacksonians, and for the past century, U.S. foreign policy seesawed between these two extremes. But during the Second World War and the Cold War, their respective supporters were allied to defeat the immoral threats that foreign dictators posed to U.S. security and values.

These threats can in part be seen to have arisen because the United States failed to establish its hegemony in 1918. On October 10, 1916, Keynes saw that financial hegemony had passed irrevocably across the Atlantic. In a memorandum to the British Treasury, he wrote, "The policy of this country towards the USA should be so directed as not only to avoid any form of reprisal or even active irritation but also to conciliate and please."[18] By then, the British were completely financially dependent on the United States.

Nor, as Keynes bitterly complained in his brilliant *The Economic Consequences of the Peace*, did Wilson succeed in fulfilling the pledge in his Fourteen Points—whose acceptance by Germany ended the war—that no Carthaginian Peace as demanded by the victors, particularly France, would be imposed on Germany. Keynes believed Wilson was bamboozled by the "Welsh witch," Lloyd George, into acceding to Clemenceau's desire to dismember German military and economic power, believing such actions were in accord with his Fourteen Points. By the time Lloyd George realized his mistake, he could not "in five days persuade the President of error in what it had taken five months to prove to him to be just and right. After all it was harder to de-bamboozle this old Presbyterian than it had been to bamboozle him; for the former involved his belief in and respect for himself."[19] But, Skidelsky rightly notes that "Keynes' criticism of Wilson's character hinged on a mistaken assessment of the President's priorities. Wilson conceded on points that Keynes thought important, but which Wilson did not."[20] This was because Wilson's main purpose was to get his League of Nations. "From Wilson's vantage point, if this League were incorporated into the general settlement, then he could feel confident that he had kept his faith, that the most important objective of the Great War had been consummated, and that any injustices done by the treaty of peace itself could be redressed later with relative ease."[21] But with Wilson's failure to persuade the Senate to accept the League, and the subsequent turn to U.S. isolationism, the flawed treaty did, as Keynes feared, lead to "the bankruptcy and decay of Europe . . . [which] will affect everyone in the long run, but perhaps not in a way that is striking or immediate."[22]

The most trenchant criticism of Wilsonian universal moralism and the idealist theory of foreign relations was provided by E. H. Carr in *The Twenty Years Crisis*, written in 1939 on the eve of World War II.[23] The League of Nations, as the realists had always maintained, proved a broken reed to maintain the peace.

After the Second World War, the United Nations resurrected this Wilsonian universal moralism. Once again, the anthropomorphic identification of states as persons and the presumption of an essential harmony of interests among these equal world "citizens" were proclaimed. Collective economic sanctions brought into line those that broke international norms. As a detailed study by Gary Huffbauer and his associates shows, these sanctions have been ineffective and inefficient in serving their foreign policy goals.[24] By contrast, the nineteenth-century British pax was not maintained through economic sanctions to change states' behavior;

instead, direct or indirect imperialism was used. The contrasting lessons from the last two centuries are of obvious relevance to the current confrontation with the "Axis of Evil" and the global "War on Terror."

II

A second important aspect of an empire's pax is the transnational legal system created for the protection of property rights, particularly those of foreigners. As Lipson shows in his brilliant study *Standing Guard*, this was due to the commercial treaties signed by European states in the mid-nineteenth century. The treaties provided rules for protecting international property rights, which "hardened into general principles of international law."[25] These international standards built upon the system of commercial law that had been established as a result of Pope Gregory VII's eleventh-century papal revolution.[26] The treaties of Westphalia (1648) and Paris (1763) further strengthened the economic rights of foreigners and their property abroad. The nineteenth century saw a culmination of this process, with the security of foreign persons and their property guaranteed by every European state, the United States (soon after its independence at the end of the eighteenth century), and the new Latin American states (after their wars of independence). This extension of the international rule of law covered what was previously Christendom in Europe and the New World, and the role of the medieval Catholic Church in providing the first "international" legal system which covered the Christian states in Europe.

Since legal systems are in part derived from people's cosmological beliefs (as I denoted them in *Unintended Consequences*), it is not surprising that this common international standard was readily adopted in lands where people had a shared cosmological heritage. Matters differed greatly when it came to areas with dissimilar cosmological beliefs in the Middle East, Asia, and Africa. Even there, the principle of reciprocity—which had partly led the European states of the Middle Ages to accede to various international standards—was also behind the Ottoman Empire's acceptance of various "capitulation" treaties dating back to the 1500s. Under these treaties, the Ottomans granted commercial privileges to the states of Christendom; in return, Muslim merchants and other subjects of the Ottomans received protection for their goods and persons abroad. The principle of reciprocal protection was directly written into the Ottoman Treaty of 1540.

With its growing economic strength and increased concern about Russian expansion in the Eastern Mediterranean, Britain signed the Anglo-Turkish convention in 1838, which effectively opened up the Ottoman Empire to European trade and investment. In time, with the growing enfeeblement of the Ottomans, new arrangements arose concerning disputes with foreigners, whereby "international property rights were effectively guaranteed by the extra territorial application of European and American laws."[27]

The European powers under British leadership found that in parts of the world where European cosmological beliefs were alien, to expand trade and investment, they had to create systems of foreign concessions and extraterritorial laws—as in the treaty ports of the Far East. Where political arrangements were fragile—as in Africa—the creation of political and legal structures to serve commercial expansion led to difficult choices for the Victorians in integrating the agricultural periphery with the dynamic industrialism of Europe and the United States.[28] "Their policies naturally aimed at a vast, global extension of commerce. At the same time, they tried to limit the direct imposition of political and military controls, which were expensive and difficult to manage."[29]

This global network of laws protecting foreign capital allowed the worldwide expansion of the "gentlemanly capitalism" of London, which Cain and Hopkins have persuasively argued was the hallmark and real motivating force behind the British Empire. This legal framework was an essential element of Pax Britannia. Together with the economic integration through free trade and an international payments system based in London, it allowed the empire to fulfill a wider mission—the world's first comprehensive

TABLE 2
A TURNING POINT CHRONOLOGY

1840	Chile	1900	Cuba
1850	Brazil	1910	Korea
1850	Malaysia	1920	Morocco
1850	Thailand	1925	Venezuela
1860	Argentina	1925	Zambia
1870	Burma	1947	India
1876	Mexico	1947	Pakistan
1880	Algeria	1949	China
1880	Japan	1950	Iran
1880	Peru	1950	Iraq
1880	Sri Lanka	1950	Turkey
1885	Colombia	1952	Egypt
1895	Taiwan	1965	Indonesia
1895	Ghana	1965	Afghanistan
1895	Ivory Coast	1965	Bangladesh
1895	Nigeria	1965	Ethiopia
1895	Kenya	1965	Mozambique
1900	Uganda	1965	Nepal
1900	Zimbabwe	1965	Sudan
1900	Tanzania	1965	Zaire
1900	Philippines		

SOURCE: Lloyd Reynolds, *Economic Growth in the Third World* (New Haven: Yale University Press, 1983), 958.

development program. After 1815, Britain aimed to establish a set of like-minded allies that would cooperate in keeping the world safe from what George Canning called the "youthful and stirring nations" (such as the United States), which proclaimed the virtues of republican democracy, and from a "league of worn out governments" in Europe, whose future lay too obviously in the past. Britain offered an alternative vision of a liberal international order bound together by mutual interest in commercial progress and underpinned by a respect for property, credit, and responsible government, preferably of the kind found at home.[30]

FIGURE 1

GDP FOR MAJOR COUNTRIES, 1500–1998, RELATIVE TO RUSSIA

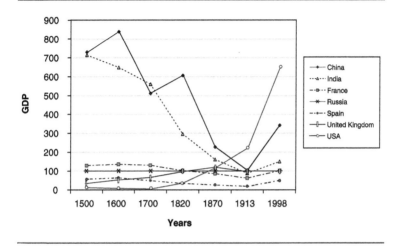

SOURCE: Angus Maddison, *The World Economy: A Millennial Perspective* (OECD, 2001), table B-18.
NOTE: Russia = 100.

Compared with the previous millennia, the results were stupendous. From 1850 to 1914—the height of this nineteenth-century LIEO—many parts of the third world for the first time experienced intensive growth for a sustained period. In his survey of the economic histories of forty-one developing countries, Lloyd Reynolds dated the turning points when developing countries entered the era of intensive growth (table 2). This era was accompanied by a sustained rise in per-capita incomes, as compared with the ubiquitous extensive growth of the past, when output growth just kept up with population growth.

The First World War marked the beginning of the end of this nineteenth-century LIEO. As shown in figure 1—which charts the relative economic strength of various potential (and actual) imperial contenders from the sixteenth century to the 1990s—it is clear that by 1914 the United States was by far the dominant economic power. But after the First World War it retreated into isolationism, and during the Great Depression (in part caused by its faulty monetary policy), the United States failed to do what Britain in the depression of the 1870s had done as the economic world leader—maintain open markets for trade and finance. The Smoot-Hawley Tariff and blue-sky laws (which banned U.S. banks from lending to foreign governments) in effect ended the LIEO.

Worse still, the turmoil of the interwar period unraveled the complex web of international law and practice the British had woven in the nineteenth century to protect foreign capital. From the start of the First World War to 1929 (when international capital markets effectively closed down), the United States was the world's largest lender. During that period, U.S. foreign investments increased sixfold so that by 1929, its stock of foreign investment equaled that of Britain. But the weakening of British hegemony meant that enforcement of the nineteenth-century international rules became problematic. As Lipson notes:

> Before [World War I], the United States had assumed responsibility for enforcing property rules only in Latin America. Elsewhere, sanctions were either British or collective. Now, however, Europe was weak and divided, and Britain was unable to act alone. The most obvious solution was condominium between the two largest investors, the United States and Great Britain. Yet President Wilson's defeat [in his attempt to bring the United States into the League of Nations] excluded that hypothetical solution. Even though US economic interests continued to expand, the state flatly refused to assume commensurate political and military responsibilities outside the Western hemisphere. That refusal and Britain's shrunken power diminished the capacity of advanced capitalist states to enforce traditional property rules.[31]

Moreover, it is doubtful that even if Wilson had succeeded in his efforts to bring the United States into the League of Nations, he would have enforced international property rights, given his socialist sympathies, his ambivalence toward the Mexican and Russian revolutions,[32] and his promotion of national self-determination (discussed below). The Mexican and Russian revolutions and the explicit introduction of statist policies by Atatürk in Turkey—the successor state to the extinguished Ottoman Empire—led to the questioning of the legitimacy of these rules. Subsequently, when faced with social policies designed to promote the nationalist weal, there was a worldwide erosion of public acceptance of the sanctity of private property rights.

The post–World War II United States—chastened by the global disorder its interwar isolationism had permitted—sought a partial restoration of the nineteenth-century international rules, but it did not extend them to the newly decolonized third world, which experienced an explosion of economic nationalism. The "embedded liberalism"[33] (another label for democratic socialism) promoted by Wilson and then Franklin Roosevelt also meant that the sanctity of property rights—which the classical liberals had always sought to further—no longer had much resonance in the domestic politics of either the United States or the United Kingdom. Given the anti-imperialist moralism of U.S. foreign policy after Wilson, attempts like the ill-fated adventure of the British and the French in 1956 to prevent Nasser's nationalization of the Suez Canal were scuttled by the United States. Thereafter, no country could stand against the new nation-states to assert its rights of national sovereignty against any purported international property rights. There was no bulwark against this disintegration of the international legal order. Most developing countries (as well as many European ones), being both nationalist and *dirigiste*, sought to regulate, tax, or nationalize particular foreign investments on the grounds of national social utility, rather than any particular antagonism to private property. This made it difficult for the United States to identify expropriation of foreign capital with a socialist ideology, as the nationalization of foreign oil companies in the 1960s and early 1970s by right-wing governments in the Middle East proved. This has cast a long shadow on the present.

But the United States did try during the Second World War (at Bretton Woods) to resurrect the three pillars on which the nineteenth-century LIEO had been built—free trade, the gold standard, and free capital mobility. But while the British Empire had fostered these pillars by example, treaties, and direct and indirect imperialism, the United States instead created transnational institutions—the General Agreement on Tariffs and Trade (GATT), followed by the World Trade Organization (WTO), the International Monetary Fund (IMF), and the World Bank.

Rather than following the successful British policy of adopting unilateral free trade and then allowing its hegemony to spread the norm, the United States has chosen the extremely acrimonious route of multilateral—and more recently, bilateral—negotiations to reduce trade barriers. The British correctly saw free trade as a non-zero-sum game and since the repeal of the Corn Laws adhered to it and its close cousin, laissez faire,[34] throughout the nineteenth century—despite various attempts by politicians like Joseph Chamberlain to stir the pot by demanding protection in the name of "fair trade." But unlike the British, the Americans never accepted the classical liberal case for free trade. They have been protectionist and always looked upon trade as a zero-sum game. Only for a brief period between 1846 and 1861 was there a relatively liberal trade policy, and even then the average ad valorem tariff on the fifty-one most imported categories of goods was 27 percent.[35] Hamilton's flawed argument for "infant industry" protection provided the original justification for protectionism.[36] But once U.S. industry had caught up with and even overtaken European industry by 1890, this argument was no longer persuasive, and the United States argued for reciprocity as the central principle of its trade policy. In his 1901 message to Congress, Theodore Roosevelt said, "Reciprocity must be treated as the handmaiden of Protection. Our first duty is to see that the protection granted by the tariff in every case where it is needed is maintained, and reciprocity be sought so far as it can be safely done without injury to our home industries."[37]

This principle of reciprocity has been the central tenet of U.S. trade policy ever since, and the late twentieth-century world leader has sought to achieve free trade through reciprocal concessions in the GATT and the WTO. But as the antiglobalization riots from Seattle onward demonstrate—by perpetuating the myth that trade is a zero-sum game and that removing tariffs can only be done on the basis of reciprocity—issues of domestic policy will inevitably spill over into trade policy.

The attempt to resurrect something similar to the gold standard (based on a quasi-fixed exchange rate system policed by the IMF) also foundered on its basic premise that while freeing trade and maintaining convertibility on the current account, the capital account could be managed by distinguishing between long-term (good) and short-term (bad) capital flows. With the freeing of trade, such capital controls were shown to be ineffective, as capital could be moved through the process of "leads and lags" in the current account. With the gradual move to floating exchange rates, the need for the policeman of the Bretton Woods system—the IMF—also disappeared. Clearly, this new international monetary system, which has been dubbed a "non-system," has the advantage for international relations that, being decentralized, it does not require international cooperation (and its potential for discord) of a fixed exchange rate system.

The World Bank was the instrument chosen to resurrect the international capital market which had been closed in particular to developing countries, due to their defaults in the 1930s. Laws were passed that forbade U.S. financial intermediaries from holding foreign government bonds.[38] But the financial intermediation role of the Bank was soon overtaken by its role as a multilateral foreign aid agency, in part to participate in the Cold War—both by tying the "non-aligned" to the free world and by promoting economic development. The World Bank was to be used to create another international development program, analogous to the one the British had promoted in the nineteenth century—through the propagation and enforcement of rules concerning international property rights, and through direct and indirect imperialism. As these routes were eschewed, the only instrument available was the use of "conditionality" tied to these flows to promote the appropriate development policies in the third world, by changing state behavior. But as with sanctions to serve foreign policy goals, this ever more stringent "conditionality" has—as shown in the detailed study by Paul Collier et al.—been unsuccessful. Thus, the current development mantra is that "good governance is all." Now the stark choice facing the successors of Wilsonian idealism in foreign policy also faces them in international economic policy: Can the order required for prosperity be promoted without direct or indirect imperialism?

III

The third purpose empires serve is to quell ethnic conflicts. President Wilson's invoking of the principle of national self-determination, as he proclaimed the new moral Age of Nations to replace the immoral Age of Empires, let the ethnic genie out of the bottle. As Dean Acheson noted in a speech at Amherst College on December 9, 1964, this lofty principle

> has a doubtful moral history. [Woodrow Wilson] used it against our enemies in the First World War to dismember the Austro-Hungarian and Ottoman Empires, with results which hardly inspire enthusiasm today. After the Second World War the doctrine was invoked against our friends in the dissolution of their colonial connections. . . . On the one occasion when the right of self-determination—then called secession—was invoked against our own government by the Confederate States of America, it was rejected with a good deal of bloodshed and moral fervor. Probably you will agree it was rightly rejected.[39]

From the viewpoint of global order, the most common form of deadly conflict today is civil war in the name of cultural self-determination. Recent research by Oxford's Paul Collier and his associates on the causes of civil wars finds that the relationship of ethno-linguistic fragmentation in a state and the risk of a civil war forms an inverted U in shape.[40] The most homogenous as well as the most fragmented states are least at risk of civil war. There is thus likely to be bipolarity in the institutions best able to deal with ethnic diversity. One (complete fragmentation) is found in empires. The other (homogeneity) is surprisingly a course Keynes advocated during the Second World War when speculating about the ideal political postwar order in Europe. Skidelsky reports on one of Keynes's fancies:

> A view of the post-war world which I find sympa-
> thetic and attractive . . . is that we should encourage
> small political and cultural units, combined into larger,
> and more or less closely knit, economic units. It would
> be a fine thing to have thirty or forty capital cities in
> Europe, each the center of a self-governing country
> entirely free from national minorities (who would be
> dealt with by migrations where necessary) and the seat
> of government and parliament and university center,
> each with their own pride and glory and their own
> characteristics and excellent gifts. But it would be
> ruinous to have thirty or forty entirely independent
> economic and currency unions.[41]

But as Skidelsky notes, "this pleasing picture of a re-medievalised Europe did not survive in later drafts."[42] This homogenized solution, which as Keynes recognized could involve "ethnic cleansing," has clearly been eschewed by the West—as witnessed by its actions in Bosnia and Kosovo. This reflects the hopes of much progressive thought over the last two centuries—stemming from the Enlightenment—that transnational and "modern" forms of association, such as class, would transcend primordial forms of association, such as ethnicity and culture (of which nationalism is an offshoot) But contemporary history continues to show the power of these primordial forces. Much-derided sociobiology provides some cogent reasons for their survival.

Evolutionary anthropologists and psychologists maintain that human nature was set during the period of evolution ending with the Stone Age.[43] One salient feature of the Stone Age environment was that rapid "species"-relevant judgments had to be made on the basis of quick impressions. Our brains, according to the evolutionary psychologists, have been hardwired to deal with the problems faced in the primordial environment—the savannahs of Africa, where judging that a dangerous predator was at hand was a matter of life and death. The decision, moreover, had to be instantaneous, without any time spent on continued sampling to confirm one's conjecture that a yellow shape with stripes in the distance was indeed a tiger. According to the evolutionary psychologists, this indicates we are naturally primed to make instantaneous "species" judgments.[44]

Given the divergence among different human groups in physiognomy and culture, once our ancestors spread throughout the world and then rarely came in contact with their genetic cousins—at the end of the Ice Age, the ice bridges linking the continents melted—it is hardly surprising that when we do come across another ethnic group, we are primed to look upon it as a different species. Intermarriage and long familiarity might change these natural instincts, but as the bloody outcome in the successor states of Yugoslavia demonstrates, any such change does not appear likely in the near future. This provides one important reason, rooted in our biology, why the Enlightenment hopes of the reduction—if not ending—of ethnic differences and conflicts have not been fulfilled.

At least in principle, the Keynes solution seems to be in keeping with human nature. As in a globalized economy, size does not matter for prosperity—demonstrated by the shining examples of the city-states of Hong Kong and Singapore. Prosperity is feasible, as long as someone maintains a global pax.

However, the events in Bosnia and Kosovo show that the United States and its allies have (rightly in my view) chosen to impose a regional pax by reconstructing parts of the Balkan Austro-Hungarian Empire. The High Representative of the UN in Bosnia, and the Chief Administrator of Kosovo are the equivalent of British viceroys in areas of direct imperialism, and political agents in those of indirect imperialism. Similarly, the recent

Afghan peace is underwritten by an allied police force—another form of indirect imperialism—much as the British sought to do through their Residents in Afghanistan during their imperium.

IV

Even if there is a case for Pax Americana to maintain global peace and protect property rights, Paul Kennedy has argued that it would lead to "imperial overstretch" and the nationalist backlash that has undermined past empires.[45] American foreign policy has tolerated such resistance in the past, but it seems unlikely that it will pose a serious challenge to the Pax Americana.

I have gathered figures on the share of military spending in gross domestic product (GDP) of the United States and other potential great powers from the late 1980s, together with their total military spending in purchasing power parity in U.S. dollars (PPP $) for 1990 and 2000 (table 3 and figure 2). The first of these shows that if there were any imperial overstretch, it was in the former Soviet Union. Even currently, its share of military expenditure in GDP remains much higher than any other country's. I then examined the GDP growth rates needed by the other great powers to achieve parity with the United States in terms of military PPP $ at various dates, assuming the U.S. PPP GDP continued to expand at the average rate of 3.3 percent, as it has done over the last twelve years. I also assumed that the shares of military expenditure in GDP of each country remained unchanged from 1990—so that none of these countries (apart perhaps from Russia) had to choose between guns and butter. Table 4 shows that based on economic performance and the current rate of military expenditures, the only countries that could catch up to the United States in military spending and become a potential competitor to American military power are China (by perhaps midcentury) and India (by the end of the century). Given the U.S. technological lead, these potential catch-up dates are likely to occur even later. It is thus unlikely that U.S. military power will be challenged, at least in this century. As discussed below,

TABLE 3

MILITARY EXPENDITURES AS A PERCENT OF GDP,
MAJOR POWERS, 1988-2000

	1988	1989	1990	1991	1992	1993
China	2.7	2.7	2.7	2.5	2.7	2.1
France	3.7	3.6	3.5	3.5	3.4	3.3
India	3.1	2.9	2.7	2.5	2.3	2.4
Russia	15.8	14.2	12.3	0.0	5.5	5.3
UK	4.1	4.1	3.9	4.2	3.8	3.5
USA	5.7	5.5	5.3	4.7	4.8	4.5
EU	1.7	1.7	1.7	1.7	1.7	1.7

	1994	1995	1996	1997	1998	1999	2000
China	1.9	1.8	1.8	1.9	2.0	2.1	2.1
France	3.3	3.1	3.0	2.9	2.8	2.7	2.6
India	2.3	2.2	2.1	2.2	2.2	2.4	2.4
Russia	5.9	4.1	3.8	4.2	3.2	3.6	4.0
UK	3.3	3.0	2.9	2.7	2.6	2.5	2.5
USA	4.1	3.8	3.5	3.3	3.1	3.0	3.1
EU	1.7	1.7	1.7	1.7	1.7	1.7	1.7

SOURCE: Stockholm International Peace Research Institute, sipri.org/contents/milap/milex/mex_database.

however, the question of whether a coalition of these potential great powers will challenge an American imperium remains.

From the experience of the British Empire, we have some idea of the administrative cost of running an empire—based on both direct and indirect imperialism. At the end of the Second World War, the elite administrative division of the colonial service in Africa—including district officers and central secretariats, but not railway, agriculture, or other specialist departments—numbered slightly more than 1,200 men, spread over more than a dozen colonies covering nearly 2 million square miles, with an estimated population

FIGURE 2
MILITARY EXPENDITURES: MAJOR POWERS, 1990 AND 2000
(billions of PPP $)

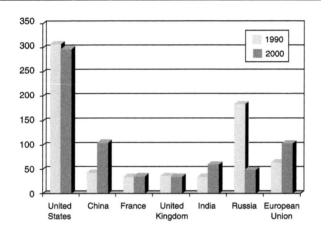

SOURCE: Stockholm International Peace Research Institute, sipri.org/contents/milap/
milex/mex_database.
NOTE: European Union includes France and the United Kingdom.

of 43 million. The Sudan Political Service, which reported to the
Foreign Office, had 125 senior officials for a territory twice
the size of Texas. For a population of 353 million, the Indian Civil
Service had a maximum strength of 1,250 covenanted members,
whereas the relatively well-manned Malayan Civil Service possessed
some 220 elite administrators for a mere 3.2 million people.[46] In
total, fewer than 3,000 civil servants from the metropolis ran the
empire. This can be compared with the huge numbers of noncleri-
cal officials in the transnational organizations—the UN, the World
Bank, the IMF, and the WTO—currently seeking to run the postwar
Wilsonian international political and economic order. (See table 5,
which does not include the 2000 World Bank officials outside
Washington and the 65,000 UN officials outside its headquarters.)

The small numbers of metropolitan civil servants were supple-
mented by a large army of English-speaking "Creoles." In India, in

TABLE 4

WHAT GROWTH RATE WOULD ENABLE COUNTRIES TO CATCH
UP WITH AMERICAN MILITARY EXPENDITURES?

	2020	2050	2100
China	8.5	5.2	4.1
France	14.3	7.4	5.2
UK	14.6	7.5	5.2
India	11.8	6.4	4.7
Russia	12.7	6.8	4.9
EU	6.5	4.4	3.7

Assumptions:
  • U.S. real PPP GDP will grow at a constant 3 percent per year (average from 1988 to 1998).
  • Military expenditures / GDP ratio will stay the same as in 2000.

SOURCE: World Development Indicators for PPP GDP in 2000, www.worldbank.org/WDI/; Stockholm International Peace Research Institute, *Database for Military Expenditures*, sipri.org/contents/milap/milex/mex_database; Angus Maddison, *The World Economy: A Millennial Perspective* (OECD, 2001), appendix C, table C 1-b.

TABLE 5

EMPLOYMENT IN MAJOR INTERNATIONAL ORGANIZATIONS

UN Headquarters	8,700
World Bank	10,000
IMF	2,650
WTO Secretariat	550
Total	21,900

SOURCE: UN website, www.un.org; World Bank website, www.worldbank.org; IMF website, www.imf.org; WTO website, www.wto.org.

his famous "Minute on Education," Lord Macaulay stated that the English wished to create an English-educated native middle class "who may be interpreters between us and the millions whom we govern; a class of persons, Indian in blood and colour, but English in taste, in opinions, in morals, and in intellect."[47] He also foresaw that this could in time lead to the creation of the class which would contest and replace British rule. Thus in the 1833 Charter Debate in the British Parliament, Macaulay said: "It may be that the public mind of India may expand under our system till it has outgrown that system, that by good government we may educate our subjects into a capacity for better government; that, having become instructed in European knowledge, they may, in some future age demand European institutions. Whether such a day will ever come I know not. But never will I attempt to avert or retard it. Whenever it comes, it will be the proudest day in English history."[48]

These "Macaulay's children," as we may call them, were to overthrow the empire. Their nationalist revolts were part of that "Creole nationalism" which, as Benedict Anderson argued, overthrew colonial rule in the Americas.[49] The major complaint of the "Creoles" against the Peninsulares (descendants of the conquistadores of the Iberian peninsula) was that, even though in almost every respect—language, descent, customs—they were indistinguishable, they had an inferior status because of the accident of their birth. In India, Macaulay's children also had an inferior status, despite being English in every respect except "blood and colour." This racism ultimately unraveled the British Empire, by fueling "Creole nationalism." But in its early phase, the British Raj had behaved like a traditional Indian power. The notions of racial exclusiveness which came to characterize its late imperial phase were alien to India's early British rulers, who exhibited a more robust delight in both the country's mores and its women. The shock of the Mutiny of 1857 and the arrival of English women turned the British in India from "nabobs" to "sahibs."

But there was another route to prevent the rise of "Creole nationalism," and this was the example of Rome, where in 212 AD, Caracalla declared all free men citizens of Rome. This meant that the Romanized elites in the provinces could and did form part of a common Roman political and social elite, and some of these non-Romans also became emperors. This Caracallan threshold, as it has been called, was never crossed by the British Empire, because of its racial exclusiveness.

One of the strengths of the United States is that, in its public and increasingly private philosophy, racism no longer plays a part—as witnessed by the fact that two of its major foreign policy leaders are African Americans. Moreover, the United States has now moved to recognizing dual citizenship, as have many other countries—with even the most nationalist like India planning to follow. With the growth of a cosmopolitan class of primarily American-trained technicians and executives (culturally and often personally linked) at work in many different countries, there already exists the core of a global "Roman" political and economic elite—open to the talents—which could run this new U.S. imperium.

V

Nevertheless, will not a U.S. imperium cause a coalition to form against it, as Christopher Layne from the Cato Institute argued recently?[50] He claims the historical record shows that hegemonic powers are likely to be challenged by a coalition of other states, for "when one state becomes more powerful—becomes a hegemon—the imbalance of power in its favor is a menace to the security of all other states."[51] Envy, jealousy, and even hatred are the inevitable and unenviable consequences of disparities in economic and military power. But should the dominant power then actively seek to become poorer and weaker so it may be loved, or to prevent other powers from "ganging up" against it in the future? Or should it instead try to use its hegemony to bring other great powers into a concert maintaining the global pax (as the British did in the nineteenth century), recognizing that its dominance will lead to emulation by many—the "soft power" idealists so often talk about—but also fear and loathing among others. Preventing the latter from spilling over into global disorder has been one of the essential tasks of imperial statesmanship. To undertake it sensibly, however, a country must recognize that it is an imperial power. Empires come before imperialism. Like other economically and militarily dominant powers in the past, the United States has acquired an empire, but it is reluctant to face the resulting imperial responsibilities because it refuses to face up to the reality in its domestic discourse. This would require the development of a theory for the beneficent exercise of its power. Wishing the empire would just go away or could be managed by global love and compassion is to bury one's head in the sand and promote global disorder.

If we look at the current threats to global or regional political and economic order, there would seem to be a convergence—rather than a divergence—in the interests of the United States and other potential great powers. There are clearly two major regions of the world where disorder rules: the vast region spanning the Islamic world in the Middle East and Central Asia, and the continent of Africa.

Sadly, with the ending of the Cold War, Africa does not represent a strategic challenge to any of the potential great powers. Its strategic importance in the nineteenth century, no longer applicable today, lay in guarding the sea lanes to India—the jewel in the British imperial crown. Apart from justified humanitarian concerns about the plight of its people, the world has little to lose or gain from Africa. Given the dismal failure of the Western development program in Africa—based on conditional aid channeled through governments run by predatory elites—little short of costly direct imperialism is likely to provide the good governance that is a prerequisite for the economic advancement of the continent.

As is already evident and lamented by these African elites, Africa will likely become increasingly marginal to the world economy and polity. Perhaps in its pursuit of ethical imperialism—as a British foreign policy advisor to Tony Blair has recommended as the EU's future foreign policy—the EU or its old imperial countries, the UK and France, will be willing to spend men and materiel to establish and maintain an imperium. This would allow Africa the period of peace and good government it needs for prosperity. But in the changed circumstances, any contemporary plea similar to that of Kings Bell and Acqua is likely to fall on deaf ears. In any case, there is no danger that a great-power coalition will form against the United States over Africa. For the United States and the world, the best policy toward Africa (if direct imperialism is too costly) is to keep markets for African goods and capital flows to Africa open and leave it to the Africans to sort out their own problems.

The Islamic world poses a more serious challenge. In rightly trying to distinguish the direct threats posed to global security after September 11 as from Islamists, not Islam—in no small measure to protect the substantial Muslim minorities in many Western countries—many commentators and world leaders have gone out of their way to say that, in the "war on terror," the enemy is not Islam. At one level this is true. Bernard Lewis, the doyen of Middle Eastern studies, once remarked to me that the Islamist threat is greater for other Muslims than it is for the West. But once one seeks to understand the reason for the rise of Islamic fundamentalism and its seeming attractiveness to large numbers in Muslim countries, it is difficult to escape the conclusion that it has something to do with the nature of Islam itself.

The best way to see the problem is to go back in time before the rise of the West. At the end of the first millennium, the dominant world civilization was that of Islam. The Syrian geographer Al-Muqaddasi described the Islamic world at the turn of the millenium: "The strict political unity which had once characterized Islam had been shattered in the tenth century . . . yet a sense of comity survived, and travelers could feel at home throughout the Dar al-Islam—or to use an image popular with poets—in a garden of Islam, cultivated, walled against the world, yielding for its privileged occupation, shades and tastes of paradise."[52]

This paradise was shattered by the rise of the West. When the Ottomans were turned back after the siege of Vienna in 1683, the Islamic world went into relative decline, and by the end of the First World War and the dismemberment of the Ottoman Empire, it was clear that Islam was a defeated civilization. This had also been true of the other great Eurasian civilizations—the Indian, the Chinese, the Japanese—when they encountered the West. These civilizations had two responses to the Western onslaught in the nineteenth century. The first was that of the oyster, which closes its shell. The other was to modernize, to try to master foreign technology and way of life, and to fight the alien culture with its own weapons. Japan is the prime example of a country which chose the latter route. India and China seesawed between the two responses and took nearly a century truly to come to terms with modernization. Some Islamic countries, in particular Atatürk's Turkey and Mehmet Ali's Egypt, also took the second route, but only partially. The other remedy, the oyster—whereby Muslims sought to regain Allah's favor by purifying Islam from the corruptions that had crept into Muslim lives over the centuries—has had much greater resonance. For deep cultural reasons I cannot go into on this occasion, the other non-Muslim civilizations have come to realize that modernization does not entail westernization, and hence ancient cosmological beliefs can be maintained, even when material beliefs have to change to modernize.[53] Yet as William McNeill notes, it was Islam's misfortune (unlike the Japanese) that despite many voices—for example, Sir Sayed Ahmad in nineteenth-century India—stating that modernity could be reconciled with Islam, "the two remedies seemed always diametrically opposed to one another. Reformers' efforts therefore tended to cancel out, leaving the mass of Muslim society more confused and frustrated than ever."[54]

Until the Muslim world wholeheartedly embraces modernization, recognizing that it does not involve westernization and the giving up of its soul, there is little hope the Islamist threat will be eliminated. But how is such a change to come about?

Consider the Middle East world created with the dismemberment of the Ottoman Empire. Apart from Egypt, Turkey, Saudi Arabia, and Iran, the rest of the states in the Middle East today are the artificial creations of the victorious powers which dismembered the Ottoman Empire. Thus Iraq, instead of being—as Saddam Hussein has claimed—the successor state of Nebuchadnezzar, was actually put together by Britain as a unit containing Kurdish, Sunni, and Shia tribes in the region. This artificial tribal confederation has always been brittle, and its unity has been maintained not by any national feeling but by tribal deals and most recently by terror.

The Kingdom of Saudi Arabia is also not the descendant of any ancient Arab state, but the result of a religious movement—the Wahabis (an extreme version of Islam) creating a state in central Arabia in the eighteenth century.[55] This state, along with Yemen, maintained its independence through the turbulent period when the British and the French held mandates over most of Palestine and the Arabian Peninsula. But, "without known resources, with few links with the outside world, and surrounded on all sides by British power, [they] . . . could be independent only within limits."[56] The discovery of small amounts of oil in the 1930s changed Saudi fortunes.

This oil was discovered, extracted, and exported by Western companies, and by 1960, the total Middle Eastern oil reserves were estimated to be about 60 percent of known world reserves. Given the erosion of international rules concerning property rights, and the growth of statism, the Saudi oil fields—along with others in Iraq and Iran—were nationalized. The Saudis were, moreover, protected by the United States.

> In 1945, Franklin Delano Roosevelt flew from Yalta to Suez, where he met King Ibn Saud aboard the US navy ship Quincy. They struck the deal that would eventually "fuel" the cold war. Saudi Arabian oil flowed to the west, matching the Soviet's reserves. In return, the US promised security to the dynasty. . . . But there was always a tension at the heart of the arrangement. On the Quincy, the King was adamant that he could not compromise on his opposition to a future state for the Jews in the Muslim land of Palestine. The US dilemma ever since has been to reconcile its backing of Israel with its protection of Saudi Arabia.[57]

September 11 finally showed the dangers in this Faustian pact. The pact concerns both money and ideology. The Saudis have maintained a tightrope act for half a century. They have balanced their alliance with the infidels and the untold riches they provide the dynasty by maintaining probably the most virulent and medieval form of Islam in their own country and using their new-found wealth to propagate it through financing mosques and Wahabi preachers around the world. The madrasas (Islamic religious schools) in Pakistan—which produced the Taliban—were all run by Wahabis. The charitable donations required of all believers have often—perhaps innocently—ended up in charities which funded Al Qaeda. The Saudis have directly and indirectly funded the mosques and madrasas which preach hatred against the infidels—the Jews, Christians, and above all, the Hindus—to young minds, who learn little if anything about the modern world. But for the Saudis to eschew or put a stop to this funding would undoubtedly create a Wahabi backlash in Saudi Arabia and end the dynasty.

For the rest of the world, the poison spread by Wahabi evangelism is becoming intolerable. Imagine if German schools only taught anti-Semitism, or those in America were just teaching the young to hate blacks. But this is what the large number of madrasas—funded by the Saudis, in Pakistan and many other countries around the world—are teaching. If there is to be an end to the "war on terror," this poisoning of the Muslim mind clearly must stop.

Numerous commentators have argued that this poison continues to spread successfully because of ongoing Arab-Israeli confrontation and the anger it arouses in the Arab street, which provides the Islamists with an unlimited supply of jehadis. Without going into the historical rights and wrongs of the issue—on which I have always believed the Arabs have a rightful grievance—there are two reasons this issue (despite Arab rhetoric) is merely another symptom of the Islamic world's failure to come to terms with modernity and of the common tactic used by the third world to externalize its domestic problems.

First, the Camp David accord brokered by President Clinton in 2000–2001 gave the Palestinians virtually everything they had requested, except the so-called "right of return." Yet Arafat turned it down and instead launched the intifada. He and every Arab government knew no Israeli government could agree to the "right of return," which in effect would involve the extinction of Israel. Apart from that, Barak had accepted almost every other Palestinian demand.

Amazingly, the "right of return" after fifty years is still a controversial issue, being kept alive by the large number of Palestinians still in refugee camps. Why do they remain there after fifty years? My family and I—along with millions of others—lost our land and property as a result of the Partition of India in 1947. We were refugees. Both the Indian and Pakistani governments provided some help, but most importantly, the refugees, after a little while, made new lives for themselves. Consequently, there are no refugee camps on both sides of the India-Pakistan border with millions demanding the "right of return."

History is never just, and economists have been right to maintain that "bygones are bygones." This is particularly important in the highly contested territory of Palestine, and it became clear to me in the late 1970s when a colleague from University College London was carrying out a dig near the Wailing Wall. He took me down and showed me layer upon layer of corpses. The ones in each layer had been killed by those above, who were in turn killed by those above them. Deciding who has the original rights to this fiercely contested territory, where might has been right for millennia, would defeat even the wisdom of Solomon. Sensibly, throughout history, losers in these continual shifts in fortune have come to terms with their losses and continued with their lives.

The Palestinians could have done the same. There was plenty of land in neighboring Arab countries to provide them housing, and given the untold oil wealth that accrued in nearby Arab states, there should have been no financial impediment to their rehabilitation. Yet fifty years later, two generations have lived in the misery of these camps, waiting for the Israeli state to be destroyed. There can be no peace on those terms with Israel. Under the circumstances, what should any Prime Minister of Israel—even an Arab—do in the face of the current intifada? I have never received an answer to this question from any Arab leader with whom I have discussed the issue.

The only solution to the Arab-Israeli problem, therefore, lies in the Muslim world's coming to terms with modernity and the other Arab states' providing both land (if needed) and resources from their oil wealth to resettle the refugees. This requires that Saudi, Syrian, and Iranian direct and indirect support for the intifada must end. The current status quo in the Middle East is untenable. The primary task of a Pax Americana must be to find ways to create a new order in the Middle East, where cosmological beliefs are preserved, but the prosperity resulting from modernity leads to the end of jihad, thus easing the confusion that has plagued the Islamic soul for over a century.

A few points can be made regarding how this is to be accomplished. Many accusingly say that any such rearrangement of the status quo would be an act of imperialism[58] and would largely be motivated by the desire to control Middle Eastern oil. I argue that, far from being objectionable, imperialism is precisely what is needed to restore order in the Middle East.

Oil remains central to both the problem and the solution for two reasons. First, despite the Greens' claims that alternative forms of energy can replace oil as the major energy source, realistically this prospect is still a long way off. For the next twenty to fifty years, oil will be required not only by the present industrial countries, but also to fuel the growth of rapidly industrializing nations like India and China. With a large part of the world's known reserves of oil and natural gas still concentrated in Saudi Arabia and Iraq, these countries remain crucial for providing this essential ingredient for global prosperity.

So far, given Franklin Roosevelt's compact with the house of Saud, the Saudis remain reliable suppliers of oil. But they now face an existential dilemma, as they can no longer maintain their fifty-year balancing act. If they side with the United States, stop funding Wahabi evangelism, and clamp down on the charities funding Al Qaeda, they are likely to be overthrown by a Wahabi rebellion. Classical liberals would agree with Norman Angell that this does not matter. The successor regime would still have to depend on sales of oil to maintain its prosperity. But if Osama—

or someone of his ilk—is the leader of this successor state, we know that prosperity means nothing to them if the withholding of oil supplies is likely to destroy the infidels. The nightmare would have been an Iraq run by Saddam and a Saudi Arabia by Osama—both equally committed to choking the West and its allies.

The Saudis' other choice is to continue to use their oil wealth to fund Wahabi fundamentalist evangelism across the globe. But the poisonous mentality this would continue to spread is equally intolerable.

Either way, it seems the Rooseveltian pact will have to be revised, if not abrogated. This is not the occasion to discuss how imperial power might reorder the Middle East to allow its people to prosper under an American pax. The question is whether the United States will have to act alone in this task of establishing a Middle Eastern pax. The countries currently threatened by the spread of Islamist hatred include Russia, China, India, and of course, embattled Israel. If the maintenance of global order in the near future means countering this Islamic fascism, clearly these potential great powers will not form a coalition against the United States. Deals will no doubt have to be cut on the side, but there is no real conflict of interest that would allow a hostile coalition to build up against the United States on this issue.

Furthermore, there is at least one of these powers (apart from Israel) whose very existence as a multiethnic empire is threatened by Islamism—India. It would seem a natural partner in any reordering of the Middle East to extinguish the extremist tendency. India was the "jewel in the crown" of the British Raj not because of its fabled wealth, but because it provided the Raj with the largest land army in the world, paid for by Indian taxes. This Indian army enforced the British pax from Suez to China. Could something similar happen again in the new imperium? India has gradually been entering into what President Bush and Prime Minister Vajpayee recently hailed as a "strategic partnership." One can draw one's own conclusions. But it does seem laudable that some in the U.S. administration may at long last be taking the imperial task seriously.

VI

There are those who still believe that moral suasion will be enough to solve the Arab-Israeli dispute, and together with the use of sanctions, bring order to the Middle East. The Europeans in particular are vociferous adherents of the Wilsonian order, with their demand for multilateral action through the UN. But this is just the usual tactic of the weak: to tie Gulliver down with a million strings so that he cannot move. In terms of military and economic power, increasingly, the Europeans are becoming second-order powers; it is unlikely that any lack of support on their part will endanger an American pax. But as they have done for fifty years, they will no doubt continue to be free riders on whatever pax is created. The fears that an assertive America will provoke an aggressive counter-coalition are exaggerated.

After September 11, despite much continuing ambivalence, the United States at long last seems to be awakening from the Wilsonian dream and realizing its unique responsibility—like the British in the nineteenth century—to maintain global order. As I have emphasized, this involves the promotion of modernization—particularly in the Muslim world—but not westernization. The continuing domestic resonance of Wilsonian idealism in U.S. foreign policy, however, has the potential to undermine this emerging pax by creating a backlash, if the required modernization is mistaken for westernization.

Given its domestic homogenizing tendencies, the United States (along with various other Western countries) is attempting to legislate its habits of the heart around the world—human rights, democracy, egalitarianism, labor, environmental standards, and so on. But its claim that it is thereby promoting universal values is unjustified.

There is an important difference between the cosmological beliefs of what became the Christian West and those of the other ancient agrarian civilizations of Eurasia.[59] Christianity has a number of distinctive features that it shares with its Semitic cousin Islam, but not entirely with its parent Judaism, and that are not to be found in any of the other great Eurasian religions. The most important is its universality. Neither the Jews nor the Hindu or Chinese civilizations had religions claiming to be universal. One could not choose to be a Hindu, Chinese, or Jew; he was born as one. This also meant that, unlike Christianity and Islam, these religions did not proselytize. Third, only the Semitic religions, being monotheistic, have also been egalitarian. Nearly all other Eurasian religions (apart from Buddhism) believed in some form of hierarchical social order. By contrast, alone among the Eurasian civilizations, the Semitic ones (though least so the Jewish) emphasized the equality of men's souls in the eyes of their monotheistic deities. Dumont has rightly characterized the resulting profound divide between the societies of Homo Aequalis, which believe all men are born equal (as the *philosophes* and the American Constitution proclaim), and those of Homo Hierarchicus, which believe no such thing.[60] The so-called universal values promoted by the West are no more than the culture-specific, proselytizing ethic of what remains at heart Western Christendom. Nor is there a necessary connection—as the West claims—between democracy and development.[61] If democracy is to be preferred as a form of government, it is not because of its instrumental value in promoting prosperity (at times it may well not), but because it promotes a different Western value—liberty. Again, many civilizations have placed social order above this value, and it would be imperialistic for the West to ask them to change their ways.

If no universal claims for cherished Western cosmological beliefs are valid, it is unlikely that they will be found acceptable by the rest of the world. If the West ties its moral crusade too closely to the emerging processes of globalization and modernization, there is a danger that there will also be a backlash against globalization. This potential cultural imperialism poses a greater threat to the acceptance of a new Pax Americana in developing countries—particularly the Muslim countries—than the unfounded fears of their cultural nationalists that the modernization promoted by globalization will lead to the erosion of cherished national cultures.[62]

Conclusions

Empires have unfairly gotten a bad name, not least in U.S. domestic politics. This is particularly unfortunate, as the world needs an American pax to provide both global peace and prosperity. The arguments that this is too costly are not convincing. If instead of this pax, however, the United States seeks to create an international moral order by attempting to legislate its "habits of the heart" through ethical imperialism, it is likely to breed disorder. The most urgent task in the new imperium is to bring the world of Islam into the modern world, without seeking to alter its soul. I have given reasons to believe the United States should be able to fulfill this imperial task. But is it willing? Given the continuing resonance of Wilsonian moralism in public discourse, I am doubtful. There must first be an acceptance in domestic politics that the United States is an imperial power. The real debate about how best to use that power could then sensibly ensue.

Notes

1. Kings Bell and Acqua to William Gladstone, November 6, 1881, Foreign Office 403/18, Public Record Office, Kew, in M. W. Doyle, *Empires* (Ithaca: Cornell University Press, 1986), 162.

2. H. Bull, *The Anarchical Society* (New York: Columbia University Press, 1977), 4.

3. P. J. Cain and A. G. Hopkins, *British Imperialism, 1699–2000* (Harlow, UK: Longman, 2002), 664.

4. W. H. McNeill, *A History of the World*, 3rd ed. (New York: Oxford University Press, 1979).

5. W. J. F. Jenner, *The Tyranny of History: The Roots of China's Crisis* (London: Penquin, 1992).

6. See L. Colley, *Britons* (New Haven: Yale University Press, 1992).

7. For a model of the predatory state which explains this rise and fall of empires, see Deepak Lal, *The Hindu Equilibrium*, vol. 1, chap. 13.2 (Oxford: Clarendon Press, 1988).

8. S. E. Finer, *The History of Government*, vol. 1 (Oxford: Oxford University Press, 1997), 34.

9. Smith did have a lot to say about the costs and benefits of colonies, particularly in North America. But colonization is only one form of direct imperialism. India, for example, was not a colony (with white settlers), but was a central part of the British Empire. Nor was all of it ruled directly. The princely states that formed a large part of the British Raj were ruled indirectly through British Political Agents assigned to the "native" rulers.

10. See P. J. Cain, "Was It Worth Having? The British Empire, 1850–1950," *Revista de Historia Economica* 16 (1998): 351–76.

11. Norman Angell, *The Great Illusion* (New York: G. P. Putnam and Sons, 1911), 302.

12. Ibid., 139.

13. In an essay written in 1886 (buried in his papers till 1968), Wilson reconciles his Burkean belief in democracy by stating, "For it is very clear that in fundamental theory socialism and democracy are almost if not

quite the one and the same. They both rest at bottom on the absolute right of the community to determine its own destiny and that of its members." Cited in T. J. Knock, *To End All Wars* (Princeton, N.J.: Princeton University Press, 1992), 7.

14. Ibid., 10.

15. Ibid.

16. Ibid., 11.

17. Ibid., 10.

18. This point is made with the quote in R. Skidelsky, *John Maynard Keynes*, vol. 1 (London: Macmillan, 1983), 325.

19. John M. Keynes, *The Economic Consequences of the Peace* (London: Macmillan, 1971), 34.

20. Skidelsky, *Keynes*, vol. 1, 395.

21. Knock, *To End All Wars*, 226.

22. Keynes, *Economic Consequences*, 188.

23. See E. H. Carr, *The Twenty Years Crisis* (London: Macmillan, 1939).

24. G. Huffbauer, J. Schott, and K. Elliot, *Economic Sanctions Reconsidered* (Washington, D.C.: Institute of International Economics, 1990); Lal, "Development and Spread."

25. Lipson notes that according to these principles, "foreigners were deemed subject to local laws, as they had been since the Middle Ages, but national jurisdiction over aliens and their property had to comply with a variety of international standards." C. Lipson, *Standing Guard* (Berkeley: University of California Press, 1985), 8.

26. See H. Berman, *Law and Revolution* (Cambridge, Mass.: Harvard University Press, 1983); Deepak Lal, *Unintended Consequences* (Cambridge, Mass.: MIT Press, 1998).

27. Lipson, *Standing Guard*, 14.

28. See A. G. Hopkins, "Property Rights and Empire Building: Britain's Annexation of Lagos, 1861," *Journal of Economic History* 40 (1980): 777–98.

29. Lipson, *Standing Guard*, 15.

30. Cain and Hopkins, *British Imperialism*, 650.

31. Lipson, *Standing Guard*, 66.

32. See Knock, *To End All Wars*, 226.

33. B. Eichengreen, *Globalizing Capital* (Princeton: Princeton University Press, 1996), 4.

34. For why even in the modern theory of trade and welfare the two should again be linked, see Deepak Lal, "Free Trade and Laissez Faire: Has the Wheel Come Full Circle?" *The World Economy* 26, no. 4 (April 2003): 471–82.

35. P. Bairoch, *Economics and World History* (Chicago: University of Chicago Press, 1993), 34.

36. For the flaws, see R. E. Baldwin, "The Case against Infant-Industry Tariff Protection," *Journal of Political Economy* 77 (May/June 1969): 295–305.

37. Bairoch, *Economics*, 36.

38. W. A. Lewis, *Growth and Fluctuations*, 1870–1913 (London: Allen and Unwin, 1978), 49.

39. Dean Acheson, "Ethics in International Relations Today," in *The Puritan Ethic in United States Foreign Policy*, ed. D. L. Larson (Princeton, N.J.: Van Nostrand, 1966), 134–35.

40. See P. Collier and A. Hoeffler, "On Economic Causes of Civil War," *Oxford Economic Papers* 50 (1998): 563–73.

41. See R. Skidelsky, *John Maynard Keynes*, vol. 3, chap. 5 (London: Macmillan, 2000), 38.

42. Ibid.

43. See R. Trivers, *Social Evolution* (Menlo Park, Calif.: Mabjamin Cummings, 1985); J. Tooby and L. Cosmides, "Evolutionary Psychology and the Generation of Culture, Part 1," *Ethology and Sociobiology* 10 (1989): 29–49; J. H. Barkow, L. Cosmides, and J. Tooby, *The Adapted Mind* (New York: Oxford University Press, 1992).

44. Some natural experiments conducted by Francisco Gil Diaz of the department of anthropology at UCLA and reported at a conference on "Norms" (Center for International Relations, UCLA, 1999) provide empirical support.

45. Paul Kennedy, *The Rise and Fall of the Great Powers* (London: Fontana Press, 1989).

46. J. W. Cole, "Colonial Rule," in *The Oxford History of the British Empire*, vol. 4, eds. J. M. Brown and W. M. Roger Louis (Oxford: Oxford University Press, 1999), 232.

47. See T. B. Macaulay, *The Complete Works of Lord Macaulay*, 12 vols. (London: Longmans, Green and Co, 1898); and Lal, *Hindu Equilibrium*, chap. 5.

48. Macaulay, *Complete Works*, vol. 11, 585–86.

49. Benedict Anderson, *Imagined Communities* (London: Verso, 1991).

50. C. Layne, "The Power Paradox," *Los Angeles Times*, October 6, 2002.

51. Ibid.

52. F. Fernandez-Armesto, *Millennium* (New York: Scribner, 1995), 35.

53. But see Lal, *Unintended Consequences*, chap. 4.

54. McNeill, *History*, 390

55. Religious reformer Muhammad ibn Abdul Wahhab (1703–92) began to preach the need for Muslims to return to the teaching of Islam as understood by the followers of Ibn Hanbal: strict obedience to the Quran and Hadidth, as they were interpreted by responsible scholars in each generation, and rejection of all that could be regarded as illegitimate innovations. The reformer made an alliance with Muhammad ibn Sau'd, ruler of a small market town, Diriyya, and this led to the formation of a state which claimed to live under the guidance of the sharia and tried to bring the pastoral tribes all around it under its guidance too. The Saudis rejected the claims of the Ottomans to be the protectors of the authentic Islam. By the first years of the nineteenth century, the armies of the new state had expanded; they had sacked the Shia shrines in southwestern Iraq and occupied the holy cities of Hejaj. A. Hourani, *A History of the Arab Peoples* (Cambridge, Mass.: Harvard University Press, 1991), 257–58.

56. Ibid., 319.

57. Giles Keppel, "The Jihad in Search of a Cause," *Financial Times*, September 2, 2002.

58. Thus Joseph Nye stated on a war with Iraq: "If the US is perceived as an imperialist power, in the region, we shall encounter an antiimperial reaction that could breed a new generation of terrorists." Joseph Nye, "Owls Are Wiser about Iraq than Hawks," *Financial Times*, October 21, 2002. Two points need to be made. First, the region has been ruled by empires for millennia, some long lasting like the Roman and the Ottoman. To think that the mere existence of an empire will in itself breed terrorism—even if it brings peace and prosperity—seems to fly against history. Second, the title of his piece seems to suggest that an imperial power has to be a hawk. The effective exercise of imperial power depends upon the circumstances, requiring behavior sometimes like a hawk, sometimes like a dove, and quite often like an owl. The failure of Nye—along with so many international-relations experts in the United States—to recognize and accept that, for good or ill, the United States is already an imperial power, leads to the confusions displayed in this and other similar articles.

59. In *Unintended Consequences*, I make an important distinction between the *material* and *cosmological* beliefs of different cultures. The former relate to beliefs about the material world, including how to make a living. The latter involve how man relates to his fellow human beings and his place in the world—in Plato's words, "how one should live." There is considerable cross-cultural evidence that while material beliefs are highly malleable, cosmological beliefs are not and are, moreover, derived from the common linguistic parent of the given culture. That is why the

modernization promoted by globalization, which requires changing material beliefs, need not require westernization, which implies a change in cosmological beliefs.

60. L. Dumont, *Homo Hierarchicus* (London: Weidenfeld and Nicholson, 1970).

61. See Deepak Lal and H. Myint, *The Political Economy of Poverty, Equity and Growth* (Oxford: Clarendon Press, 1996).

62. See Lal, *Unintended Consequences*; Lal, "Cultural Self-Determination"; and Lal, "Globalisation."

About the Author

Deepak Lal is James S. Coleman Professor of International Development Studies at the University of California–Los Angeles and Professor Emeritus of Political Economy at University College in London. He has been a member of the Indian Foreign Service; a lecturer at Jesus College and Christ Church College, Oxford; and a professor of political economy at the University of London. He has served as a consultant to the Indian Planning Commission, the United Nations Conference on Trade and Development, the Organisation for Economic Co-operation and Development, the World Bank, and the ministries of planning in Korea and Sri Lanka. During the 1990s, he was codirector of the Trade Policy Unit at the Center for Policy Studies and the chairman of the board of advisors for the Nestle Lecture on the developing world.

Professor Lal is the author of numerous articles and books on economic development and public policy, including *Methods of Project Analysis* (1974); *Men and Machines* (1978); *Prices for Planning* (1980); *The Poverty of "Development Economics"* (1983, 1997); *Labour and Poverty in Kenya* (with Paul Collier, 1986); *The Hindu Equilibrium* (1988, 1989); and *The Political Economy of Poverty, Equity and Growth* (with H. Myint, 1996). Three collections of his essays have been published: *The Repressed Economy* (1993), *Against Dirigisme* (1994), and *Unfinished Business* (1999). His book *In Praise of Empires* is to be published in 2004.